PRICKLY POEMS

PRICKLY POEMS

In association with the
BRITISH HEDGEHOG PRESERVATION SOCIETY

HUTCHINSON

London Sydney Auckland Johannesburg

First published in 1992 by Hutchinson Children's Books
an imprint of the Random Century Group Ltd
20 Vauxhall Bridge Road, London SW1V 2SA

Random Century Australia (Pty) Ltd
20 Alfred Street, Milsons Point, Sydney, NSW 2061, Australia

Random Century New Zealand Ltd
18 Poland Road, Glenfield, Auckland 10, New Zealand

Random Century South Africa (Pty) Ltd
PO Box 337, Bergvlei 2012, South Africa

Designed by Paul Welti
Printed in Hong Kong
Typeset by Creative Text Limited
in 13/15pt Horley Old Style

British Library Cataloguing in Publication Data is available.
ISBN 0 09176379 7

CONTENTS

INTRODUCTION

by the British Hedgehog Preservation Society

The Hedgehog

The hedgehog has existed in pretty much its present form for about fifteen million years. The British Isles is home to the European hedgehog (Erinaceus europaeus), while other species are native to southern Europe, Africa and Asia. Though none are found in the Americas, Canada or Australia, the European hedgehog was introduced to New Zealand earlier this century and has continued to thrive there.

Hedgehogs are quite unmistakeable because of their characteristic spines. These 25mm prickles are equivalent to hairs on a human, and are lost and replaced in the same way. An adult has an average of 7,000 spines. Hedgehog feet have five toes with sharp claws for digging. They have very poor eyesight, and depend largely on their acute sense of smell for their perception of their surroundings. Their ears, though small, are also very sensitive. A hedgehog's voice is usually a snuffle (particularly when foraging), but loud snorting noises occur during courtship. Baby hedgehogs make shrill, chirping sounds, rather like birds, if they are in distress.

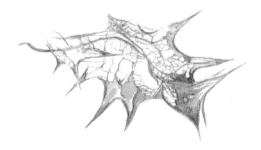

Hedgehog Lifestyle

Hedgehogs' favourite places are hedgerows, woodland, shrubberies and the wild parts of gardens and orchards where they can find nest-building materials. They also flourish in the green areas of cities. They are nocturnal creatures and may travel two miles a night in search of food, snaffling up slugs, beetles, woodlice, caterpillars and food left out for them by kind humans. In very cold weather, when their source of natural food dries up, hedgehogs go into hibernation. This is not a kind of deep sleep, but a way of conserving energy; their temperature cools down, their heartbeat decreases and breathing almost stops.

Hedgehog Families

There is no evidence of pair bonding between male and female, and most hedgehogs lead a solitary life. Litters of between four and seven are born in June or July, but if a female loses her litter, she may well produce another one in late summer. These late babies are often found wandering around in autumn, sometimes by day, far too underweight to survive hibernation. If a young hedgehog (known as a 'hoglet') does not weigh at least 500 gms it does not have enough fat in reserve. It should not be allowed to hibernate but should be kept warm and fed until spring when it can be released.

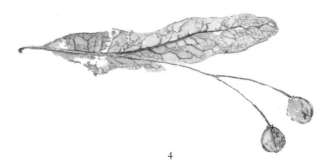

Helping Hedgehogs

There are many things everybody can do to help hedgehogs and other wildlife. For example we can:

a) stop using harmful garden chemicals and slug pellets.

b) put escape ramps in garden ponds. Hedgehogs are good swimmers, but often cannot climb out of the steep sides of most ponds.

c) try not to drop litter such as yoghurt pots and the plastic rings used for holding four-packs.

d) leave a 'wild' area in the garden. Hedgehogs eat garden pests such as slugs, beetles, and caterpillars; they do no harm themselves so they should be encouraged.

e) check heaps of garden rubbish before they're moved and bonfires before setting light to them to ensure there are no hibernating hedgehogs inside them. If a hibernating hedgehog is accidentally unearthed, it should be gently removed on a spade to a garden shed and allowed to continue its hibernation in a box filled with straw or hay.

f) leave out food and water, particularly in late summer, to help hedgehogs build up the extra layer of fat needed to survive hibernation. Hedgehogs are fond of bread and milk, but cannot digest the lactose in cow's milk and this can give them diarrhoea. Water and cat or dog food are better supplements to their normal diet. Hoglets should be given goat's milk and milk substitute baby foods.

The British Hedgehog Preservation Society

In 1982 Major Adrian Coles of Knowbury, Shropshire, rescued a hedgehog which was trapped in the cattle grid on his drive. The hedgehog would never have managed to escape without help, and would probably have died in the cattle grid of starvation. Following this incident, the Major launched a successful campaign to have ramps installed in every cattle grid in his county, for any trapped hedgehog or other wildlife to be able to climb up to safety.

He then publicised this action to encourage other county councils to follow suit. The response from the public was tremendous. Clearly, although hedgehogs had been largely ignored in the past, people now wanted to know all about them. So the British Hedgehog Preservation Society was founded and was set up in a room in Major Coles' house. It is still run from there today, and has become a respected authority on hedgehogs with a membership of over 11,000.

The Society's aims are:

1) to encourage and give advice on the care of hedgehogs, especially when injured, sick, orphaned or in distress.

2) to foster children's interest in hedgehogs with information and lectures, and thus encourage them to respect all wildlife.

3) to fund research into the behavioural habits of hedgehogs and to find out ways of aiding their survival.

This important research has been carried out by Dr Pat Morris at London University, using such methods as radio tracking and surveys. The BHPS has passed on the results to the public through its newsletters, lectures and leaflets.

Another important aspect of the BHPS's work is maintaining records of its network of volunteer hedgehog carers throughout the country.

The BHPS is delighted to be celebrating its first decade with this very special anthology of hedgehog poems, and extend our warm thanks to Hutchinson Children's Books who, by donating the royalties from the sale of each book, is aiding the Society in its work to promote the humble hedgehog.

If you would like to join the BHPS please write to:

British Hedgehog Preservation Society
Knowbury House
Knowbury
Ludlow
Shropshire SY8 3LQ

Roadhogs

Help! Watch out! Get off the road!
Hedgehogs hate the Highway Code.
At 90 miles an hour they roar
Down streets where it's against the law
To bring a car or ride a bike.
Hedgehogs do whatever they like.

And after their annual Bristle Ball
You may hear the vengeful call,
'Squash unwary humans flat!'
(They make a satisfying splat.)

So think of hedgehogs when you drive.
Like you, they'd rather stay alive.

PAUL SIDEY

French hedgehog

Who battles in Kent jardin nets?
Who fights le strangletwine?
Who stumbles in the cattle grids?
Who makes le chien whine?

Who picnics en the motorway?
Qui eats les escargots?
Who likes a fast lane walkabout?
Who rides the midnight trail?

Who walks without a safety code?
Who snorts the channel way?
His nom est Monsieur Herisson
    just come
        from France
        today.

PIERRE DIXON

Feeding the cats

'I'll give this gravy to the cats,'
  I heard my mother say
in the dark outside the kitchen door;
  but the gravy went astray:
the scrubbing brush she spilt it on
  got up and walked away.

'I hope it's got some friends,' Mum said,
  'or perhaps some babies, who
can get their tongues between the prickles –
  a tricky thing to do.
In future when I feed the cats
  I'll feed the hedgehogs too.'

FLEUR ADCOCK

I never knew

I never knew
a crown of thorns
could curl itself
into a ball

I never knew
a hairbrush
could breathe in
and out

I never knew
a nest of needles
could sprout
a beady nose
and actually move

Not until I lifted
that old carpet
beside the garden shed
and met HEDGEHOG
my bristling brother.

JOHN AGARD

Bad design

A hedgehog misses
children's kisses
their cuddles, coddles, tickles.
Rabbits or mice
seem twice as nice
designed without the prickles.

A nasty, porcupiney skin
will not allow a tickle in –
so tickles, kisses, cuddles, coddles
go to all the furry models.

JEZ ALBOROUGH

The hedgehog's valentine

If you're
sickly,
feeling
prickly,
as your
trickly
tears fall
thickly,
don't act
fickly,
kiss me
quickly –
you'll feel
tickly,
not so
prickly,
and par-
tickly
far from
sickly.

COLIN WEST

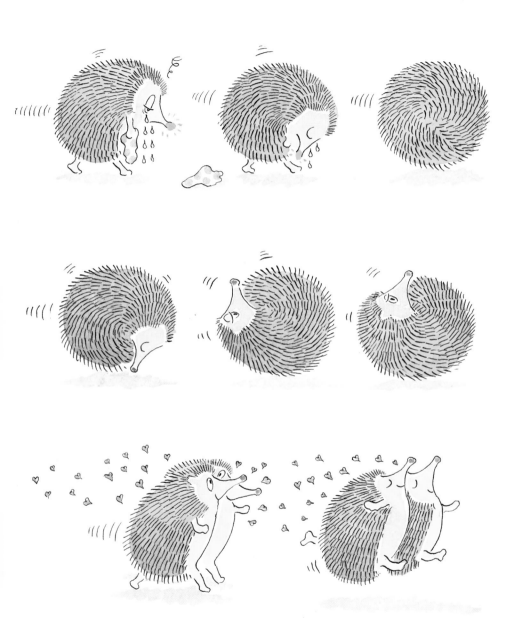

Hedgehog

They say
He's prickly and his quills hurt,
But I've stroked one many
a time,
And I don't think so!

They say he's a pest,
But he's a garden's friend
Because he eats all the bad creepy
crawlies!

They say
He's slow,
But I don't think so,
For you should see him go.

JONATHAN LLOYD, AGED 9

Hedgepodge pie

Henry was a Hedgepodge,
He loved his milk and bread.
He used to sit on people's steps
Demanding to be fed.
Instead of eating worms and bugs
And earwigs and things,
He used to ask for apple pies
And jammy, donut rings.
He even used to steal the cream
They left out for the cat.
And as he did not exercise
He started to get fat.
Soon he found it rather hard
To curl into a ball;
The little gap beneath the fence
Was suddenly too small.
A midnight mole discovered him
One windy autumn night,
Wedged beneath the wooden slats
Poor Henry was stuck tight.
With frantic scrabbling spade-like paws
The mole dug Henry out.
'Too much pie and cake,' it squealed
'Has made you far too stout.'
He led him to the garden shed
And there were mice and voles
And weasels who were overweight
All doing forward rolls.
And jumping over flower pots
And running on the spot.
Henry tried to touch his toes
And found that he could not.

Every night he practised
In the corner of the gym,
On his caterpillar diet
Henry started to get slim.
Now he's feeling fit again
So please, for goodness' sake,
No matter how a Hedgepodge pleads
Don't ever give him cake.

JEANNE WILLIS

The gardener's song

Look, here he come a-visiting
My bristle brush, my mate,
Up from the privet hedge
To my breakfast plate.
Here he come a-trundling
On his jacked-up legs,
Past our Megan's washing
And the string bag full of pegs.
And I'm glad to see thee Mister,
Good morning to you,
With your hunched back full of arrows
And your nose in the dew.
Don't need no invitation
To pleasure my eye,
Come up and see me any time
My hedgerow Samurai.

GARETH OWEN

Moving

The van has gone.
The notice saying SOLD
Is taken down.
The family, weary, strained,
Begins to settle,
Uncomfortable, into the house
Not yet their home.
Tear-stained and lonely,
The youngest boy escapes
Into the garden,
Presses his back for comfort
Against the plum tree's
Blackly knobbled bark.

> A splutter of dry leaves,
> A shiver through the long grass,
> And then the hedgehog comes.
> Scuttering, uncertain,
> Pushing through the daisies
> A mere heart's beat away.
> It stops, nose twitching,
> Scents the evening air –
> And rests a moment,
> Still, and unafraid.

The boy watches,
Smiles, and feels his pain
Retreat. 'Alright,'
He thinks. 'This place will be
Alright. Perhaps ...
I'll LIKE it here.'

JENNIFER CURRY

Chip-hog

Hog-of-the-road,
leaf-scuffer,
little tramp of the lanes –

like the old bearded one
wheel-wobbling his bicycle,
weighed to the saddle
with string bags, ropes,
a rosary of tin mugs,
or hunkered down for the winter
under threadbare thatch.

Pin-cushion,
boot-brush,
flea-bag,
eye-in-the-leafpile.

One fifth of November,
we lifted him just in time,
safe on a shovel from the smoke
of his smouldering house,
his spines sparking like stars.

Milk-scrounger,
slug-scavenger,
haunter of back doors and bins.

Once, kissing goodnight at the gate,
we saw a ghost:
something white, something small, something scratching,
headlong, hellbent, heel-over-tip hedgehog,
head in a chip-bag and hooked
on his own prickles,
the last chip escaping him
as fast as he could run.

GILLIAN CLARKE

Hedgehog hiding in harvest hills above Monmouth

Where you hide
            moon-striped grass ripples like tiger skin
where you hide
            the dry ditch rustles with crickets

where you hide
            the electricity pylon saws and sighs
            and the combine harvester's headlight
            pierces the hedges

where you hide

        in your ball of silence
        your snorts muffled
        your squeaks and scuffles
        gone dumb

        a foggy moon sails over your head,
        the stars are nipped in the bud

where you hide

        you hear the white-faced owl hunting
        you count the teeth of the fox.

HELEN DUNMORE

What did they tell you?

Did you see me first
On your mother's knee,
In a small square book,
In mob-cap and apron,
Called by a silly name?

Then again, on the road
Did you see me, squashed like a toad?
Did somebody joke?
Did you wonder why
They laugh when I die,
Not cry?

Did you hear of my prickles,
Ridden with fleas?
Did they say, when the brown cow
Sinks to her knees,
I steal her warm milk?
Did they tell you in winter
I roll in a ball?
Did you search and call?

Then, one crisp night,
By the street lamp-light,
Did something move,
Snuffle and shove
A soft snout in and out
Of the curling leaves?

Did you scarcely breathe?
Did you creep, little by little?
But, when you came where I was,
Was I gone?

Did nobody tell you
How I can run?

GINA WILSON

31

Hedgehog

is a tramp, a vagrant,
a bag-man, a cadger, a scrounger,
a dodger, a dusty old traveller,
who stumps down the lanes
and dosses in ditches
wound up in the leaves
in his flea-bitten coat.

A hedgehog's a nose
for a bite to eat, a hand-me-out
at the garden gate.
He grunts like a drunk
when he comes in late:
a great snuffle-kerfuffle
as loud as a dog
as he stumbles about
his dinner-plate.

He's a drifter, a loafer,
a poacher, a hobo, a no-go
roll-over touch-me-not waster,
unshaven and brazen
and canny of eye.
If he knocks at your door
as he passes by
you'd do well to oblige
with a sleeping-place.
For his poverty
could be you or me.
And the autumn night
with its white-clear light
is as sharp as the stars
in his crinkled face.

STUART HENSON

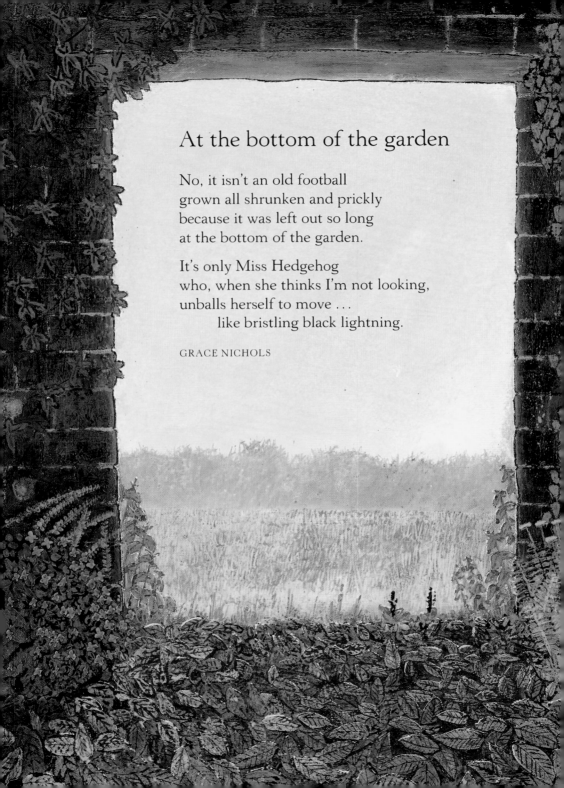

At the bottom of the garden

No, it isn't an old football
grown all shrunken and prickly
because it was left out so long
at the bottom of the garden.

It's only Miss Hedgehog
who, when she thinks I'm not looking,
unballs herself to move . . .
         like bristling black lightning.

GRACE NICHOLS

Nightwatch

This was the garden: a square of grass,
Two plastic bins, Dad's den (a shed),
A swing for the kids, a concrete path,
A washing line, and a flower bed.

This was the garden of every day.
It wasn't the garden the hedgehog knew –
For by night it changed, in a magic way,
As if it was washed in bionic dew.

The Milky Way stretched its starry banner,
Lighting the scene – for his eyes were dim –
He hunted slugs on a wide savannah,
So huge the lawn appeared to him.

The kitchen cat had changed her nature,
Sat and screamed on the moonlit wall.
The hedgehog dreaded this crazy creature,
Rolled himself in a prickly ball;

Poked out his nose, and peered morosely
Just as an owl skimmed overhead,
Floating on wings that were silent, ghostly,
Linking the living with the dead.

The swing that hung from the old crab apple
Moved very slightly, without a draught.
Something was making the moonbeams dapple
Hide and seek up the garden path.

Hedgehogs know what they know. He gobbled,
Gardening pests were his greatest feast.
Then, to his nest he slowly toddled.
He was a solitary beast.

Shut his eyes because day was coming,
Buried in leaves his hairy face,
While all around him, light was running
Into the world, from the wells of space.

JOSEPHINE POOLE

Morning meeting

Fresh dewfall glistens on the lawn;
Roses gleam with tiny pearls;
In the breeze and morning sun
Each petal trembles and uncurls;
Now in the borders all the flowers
Display their charms like dancing girls.

Then I see beside a show
Of bright nasturtiums on the ground

That curious shape: I do not know
How it came or what I've found.
Edging closer then I see

How like the bristles of a brush
Employed for scrubbing floors it looks.
'Do not touch,' it seems to say,
'Great human creature who could crush
Every small insectivore!'
'Have no fear; I'll go away
Only to come back with sweet
Greens and meat for you to eat.'

VERNON SCANNELL

Hedgehog dances

Underneath the pale magenta moon,
Hedgehog dances to a slow, sad tune
Played by an armadillo band
Sitting on their haunches
In the soft, white sand.

Hedgehog dances
In a circle on the shore,
Holding up his spiny head,
Dabbing with his paw,
Winding as a question mark,
Mournful as a sigh,
Gazing up into the moon
With brightly eager eyes.

'Moon, I love you!' Hedgehog sings.
'Moon I want you near!'
But moon just goes on shining bright
And doesn't seem to hear.

Hedgehog on the long, white beach
Dances out his love,
Moon is silent silver
In the starry sky above.

ANDREW MATTHEWS

After school

It is the end of a school day
   and down the long drive
come bag-swinging, shouting children.
   Deafened, the sun winces.
     The sky gapes in surprise.

Suddenly the runners skid to a halt,
   then stand still and stare
at a small hedgehog
   lying curled on the tarmac
     like an old, frayed cricket ball.

A girl dumps her bag, tiptoes forward
   and gingerly, so gingerly
carries the creature at arm's length
   to the safety of a shady hedge.
     She stands back, watching.

Children, sun, sky, girl,
   and trees hold their breath.
There is silence, a quiet moment
   for each to savour and remember
     on this warm afternoon in June.

WES MAGEE

Why **did** the hedgehog cross the road?

Spurned by his girlie
Rodger the hedgehog
Was suicidally blue.

Decided to bung himself under a truck
On a stretch of the M62.

SPLAT!
'What was *that?*'
The driver cried out,
As he heard a hideous squeal –

Yes – broken in body and broken in heart
Rodger was under his wheel.

He gasped and then theorised:
'Merely bad luck?
Or was it in some way intentional?'

But the only thing
He *empirically* knew
Was that Rodger was now two-dimensional.

TONY SLATTERY

The snail's lament

A hedgehog crunched a snail to bits,
And made me really MAD!
For what to him was just a snack,
To me was dear old Dad.

MIKE RATNETT

Pity hedgehogs

From their noses to their kneeses
Hedgehogs *pullulate* with fleases.
Have you spotted what the catch is?
How the dickens do they scratches?

In amongst the spikes and prickles
How those fleases bites and tickles,
But if hedgehogs scratch with clawses
They may perforate their pawses.

Pity hedgehogs, with their itches,
It's no wonder how they twitches,
When they cuddles, brushing bristles,
Love must be like kissing thistles.

ROWENA SOMMERVILLE

Only a game

From Surrey to Sunderland,
In towns small and great,
The young dream of Wonderland.
(But read Chapter Eight.)

It's not at all jokey,
You're in for a shock:
The way they play croquet
Will make your knees knock.

What fun for sweet Alice!
A creature that crawls,
A game played with malice,
And hedgehogs for balls.

It's only a story,
I hear you exclaim,
But what is most gory
Is more than a game.

Life couldn't be tougher
For hedgehogs, you see,
And those who will suffer
Will be you and me.

ROGER WODDIS

Chosen

Banging hard the back door,
Bitter I went,
Looking for trouble,
Out of my element.

*   *   *

Armed against bindweed
And knotgrass roots;
Cursing the spread of seed,
I tug on cold boots.

Gush goes a bubbling slug,
Crack goes a snail,
Smash goes a rotten log;
Wounded woodlice flail.

Guilty but glad I fork
Fierce by the wall,
Feeling the earth return
Nothing at all.

Under my pressure
Green yields to brown
Wet towers of tangled leaves
Tumble down.

Savage I drag my scalps
On to the rubbish heap,
Dreaming of firecrack
And thick smokeleap.

Conquests of seasons past
Give under my heel.
Years of unfinished feud
Are what I feel.

Then from under dead leaves
To freeze my blood
Something is stirring –
A pulsing tussock, a living sod!

Down from the heap I jump
All agog!
Slowly I register
Hedgehog.

Hedgehog? *Here?* In this place?
In *our* back yard?
Back to the house I run
Breathing hard.

Sulky, the children
Swear they will be frozen,
But warm to my wonder
That we have been chosen.

IAN WHYBROW

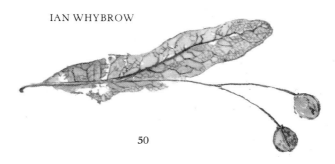

Hard hearts and hedgehogs

Cruelty is the worst heart-hardener.
When I was a kid we stayed in a house
where the gardener

had squashed a mother hedgehog flat
with the tennis court roller ...
a day or two after that

we found the three little hedgehogs, dead.
Missing their mother's milk,
they died of starvation, my mother said.

So if you see anybody being unkind
to, or hurting, a hedgehog – tell somebody!
Cruel people don't mind. But *we* certainly mind!

GAVIN EWART

Hedgehog

The road is slick
in the rain
and good slugs
can be nuzzled
out of shadows
under hedgerows.

I understand.

It's plain
you can't hurry across
even when those other lights
come at you
preceding
the hurtling mountain.

JO SHAPCOTT

The gourmet hedgehog eats out

I am a gourmet hedgehog
And I'm going out to eat.
I really like this restaurant,
It's really up my street.

I think I'll start with earwig tart –
No, wait! I'm being hasty,
Perhaps I'll try the beetle pie,
Yes, that sounds really tasty.

Now, shall I go for slugs or bugs?
The slugs are slightly sweeter.
Woodlice wine! Oh, how divine!
I think I'll have a litre.

Spicey spider lightly fried or
Maggot vindaloo?
Maggot? Spider? Can't decide.
I'd better have the two.

I've had enough. I mustn't stuff.
To eat more would be folly.
I'll simply pay and go away.
Oh no! The pudding trolley!

There's earthworm cake, for heaven's sake!
And that's my favourite sweet!
Ah, what the heck! I'll pay by cheque,
I owe myself a treat.

I really like this restaurant,
It's really up my street.
I'll come again tomorrow night
And have some more to eat.

KAYE UMANSKY

H25

Hedgehogs hog the hedges,
roadhogs hog the roads:
I'd like to build a motorway
for badgers, frogs and toads,
with halts for hungry hedgehogs
at an all-night service station;
four lanes wide and free from man
right across the nation.
Free from oil and petrol fumes,
and free from motorcars,
to see the busy hedgehogs trot
underneath the stars.

ADRIAN HENRI

Hedgehog

Watch out watch out
Hedgehog on the road
Careful all those lorries
With their heavy load

Hedgehog Hedgehog
Careful in the lane
Remember the big lorries?
Well here they come again

Careful when you're crossing
Rabbit, Frog or Toad
Remember little Hedgehog
There's danger on the road

There's the sorry Pussy
Got run over flat
So careful little Hedgehog
Or you'll end up a mat.

SPIKE MILLIGAN

They laughed

They laughed at me
Waiting under the cold stars,
Lying in the dew grass,
Listening for your rustle.
They laughed at me
Setting down the baby's milk,
Then, still as a tree,
Watching ...
But you came
And they weren't close
To the slow secret wildness of you,
Teaching me,
At a start,
How to curl inside a coat of spines
When they laugh.

ANGELA MCALLISTER

Hans my hedgehog

O I was born of a woman's wish,
　　Against the law of nature.
A child she'd sought; myself she got,
　　Half human and half creature.

For seven years long behind the stove
　　I lodged, no neighbours knowing.
They gave me straw; they gave not love.
By fairy law 'twas time to move.
　　I set about my going.

'Father fetch me what I need;
　　no longer am I staying.
Bring me a cock to be my steed,
　　And bagpipes for my playing.'

My steed and I flew high and high –
　　A treetop now my dwelling.
The woodmen stopped, amazed to hear
The sound of piping, wild and drear.
　　My story it was telling.

A king went hunting; lost and lone,
　　Cried: 'Darkness hides all traces!
A mad thing bides here, I've been told.
There's coin of gold if he'll unfold
　　The riddle of these mazes.'

'Be cheerful, King; good news I bring.
　　Hans Hedgehog is not crazy.
I see the whole world from my tree,
　　And the palace path is easy.

No gold I seek; yet hear me speak,
    I'll tell you of my feeing:
The last tree passed, mine is the first
    Live creature you'll be seeing.'

The king agreed; ''Twill be,' thought he,
    A cur, a swine, a porter.'
Ah, even kings must not ignore
The timeless ways of fairy law!
    It was his own dear daughter.

A princess true, full well *she* knew
    The laws she should be heeding.
She did not weep; she did not rail;
She did not fail the fairy tale
    And bells rang for the wedding.

I told a secret I had kept
    Through years of joy and sorrow.
They burned my beast-skin as I slept.
Hans Hedgehog to the bride-bed stepped;
    Hans Prince rose tall the morrow.

From royal bed came royal line –
    Such is the law of nature.
But half were of the hedgehog kind,
    And half the human creature.

And so the hedgehog seeks the man,
    And man his kindred creature.
To heed his need he must not fail.
Such is the law of fairy tale,
    And the true law of nature.

O listen, listen: near the ground,
  Under the dead-leaf smother,
Thin, thin, the bagpipes sound;
Light the rustling in the mound
  As the hedgehog seeks his brother.

NAOMI LEWIS

The story running through this poem is based
on 'Hans my hedgehog', one of the strangest
and most haunting of Grimms' fairy tales. The
ending here is not in the Grimms' version, but
it grows out of it quite naturally. All the best
myths and fairy tales, however odd and wild,
have inside them several secret truths that
belong to the reader's now – whenever that
now might be. What is here? The need for care
when wishing? The true closeness of human
and animal creatures? You can find others too.

Prickly friend

There's a hedgehog in the garden – come and see.
When he's still, he's like a pincushion that breathes.
When he moves, he's like a fat freckled mouse, following me
All over the place with pitter-patter feet.
He snorts and snuffs and sniffs my shoe,
Then hauls himself over the rise.

We'll introduce him to the cat. But she runs away
Into the box-tree, all hidden save her eyes
And nose and twitching tail –
Then suddenly leaps out and pounces.
(Can you blame her? He's drunk all
Her saucerful of milk, three fluid ounces.)

Caught?
Not likely. She pulls up short
And dances and prances and saws
The air all round him, mighty dainty with her paws;
Then, defeated, slinks away
To sulk or chase less prickly prey.

It's chilly now and getting late.
We'll cover him with a pile of autumn leaves
And let him hide or even hibernate.
In the morning we'll creep
Over the lawn and part the leaves and peer
Inside, and see if he's lying there asleep.
I hope he is . . .

He wasn't. He was out of his heap,
Waiting for me – wide awake perhaps all night? –
And came running towards me and round me and after me
All over the place with pitter-patter feet.

Now, were I the kind of poet
Who liked to preach
Of earth and man and animal bound each to each,
I'd draw the moral here: *We two, travellers together*
Hand in hand through life's journey
To an unknown end – would we could know it! ...
Hand in hand? Ugh, those prickles! Thank you,
I prefer to keep my distance, to stay awhile,
To watch, enjoy my play awhile,
Then leave him to it.

IAN SERRAILLIER